Also by George Ortega

Exploring the Illusion of Free Will, Second Edition

FREE WILL:
ITS REFUTATION, SOCIETAL COST AND ROLE IN CLIMATE CHANGE DENIAL

GEORGE ORTEGA

A Happier World
White Plains, New York

Published in the United States of America
for A Happier World, White Plains, New York
by CreateSpace, April 2014
Cover photo courtesy NASA
Cover design by George Ortega

10 9 8 7 6 5 4 3 2 1
Free Will and Determinism
Ortega, George 1957

ISBN-13:978-1499167641
ISBN-10:1499167644

For future generations of scientists who will likely lead our world to accept the causal nature of human will, and engineer a profoundly new and evolved civilization predicated on maximizing the benefits to humanity of understanding the far-reaching implications of this powerful, essential truth.

FREE WILL:

ITS REFUTATION, SOCIETAL COST AND ROLE IN CLIMATE CHANGE DENIAL

TABLE OF CONTENTS

1. Outline

The question of whether humans have a free will is no small matter. Searle (qtd. in Blackmore 2005) asserts that for our world to acknowledge free will as an illusion would represent "a bigger revolution in our thinking than Einstein, or Copernicus, or Newton, or Galileo, or Darwin — it would alter our whole conception of our relation with the universe." (p. 206). The traditional challenge to free will comes from determinism in the sense that nature is fundamentally causal, and causal antecedents to a human decision regress back to before the decider's birth. Psychologists like Baumeister (2008) claim that determinism has not been, nor can it be, proved, and philosophers like Mele (2012) contend that free will has not been disproved by science. While science deals with levels of confidence rather than *proof*, I argue that science evidences the causality at the heart of determinism and refutes free will with a level of confidence comparable to our knowledge that the universe exists, and that it is in constant motion.

Free will is prohibited by a causal principle that is (a) universal and a priori, (b) necessary to quantum mechanical prediction, (c) required by the law of conservation of momentum, (d) necessary to the scientific method, and (e) a result of the Heisenberg Uncertainty Principle (HUP), and evident in simultaneous particle position and momentum measurement. Mechanisms put forth as alternatives to determinism, and labeled as indeterministic, random, acausal, causa sui, ex nihilo, probabilistic, and numinous, either prohibit free will even more strongly, or are, in actuality, fundamentally causal.

After describing the above refutations, I apply them to free will defenses advanced in four articles, (Baumeister, 2008; Fingarette, 2008; Mele 2012; Meyer, 2011) reiterating them relative to the relevant contexts. Because terms like determinism, indeterminism and free will have various meanings, for clarity and accuracy I directly quote, especially in representing the authors' free will arguments. As empirical evidence against free will mounted, (Libet, Gleason, Wright and Pearl, 1983; Bargh, Chen and Burrows, 1996; Wegner, 2002; Soon, Brass, Heinze, Haynes, et al., 2008) researchers like Vohs and Schooler (2008) became concerned that disbelief in free will may be harmful. I challenge their methodology, and posit that free will belief likely causes more harm than good, especially as a catalyst for climate change denial.

2. Causality and Human Will

Refuting free will is straightforward: (a) Everything is caused; (b) Human thoughts are caused; (c) The antecedent causes to human thoughts regress to before the person's birth; (d) Therefore human thoughts are not fundamentally attributable to a human free will. Some free will defenses assume that demonstrating that human behavior is not fundamentally deterministic might provide an opening for free will, however, choices arising from indeterministic, or uncaused, processes cannot rationally be attributed to *anything*, including humans. The prospect has emerged that other mechanisms that are described as neither deterministic nor indeterministic, and can be labeled causa sui, (self-caused) or ex nihilo, (out of nothing) may be where a free will resides. However, as Strawson (1994) explains, it has not been shown how a self-caused mechanism allows for free will, and the same can be said for free will arising ex nihilo.

While Newton (1687/2010) invoked determinism to explain the motion of objects, much of the confusion today over whether determinism refutes free will stems from equating the causality manifested in determinism with the correlate of prediction. Laplace (1814/2007) described this causal principle, asserting that "present events are connected with preceding ones by a tie based upon the evident principle that a thing cannot occur without a cause which produces it." (p. 3). What created much of the current confusion was that he then went on to describe the complete knowledge of the past and prediction of the future that is the theoretically logical correlate of causality. In essence, he wrote that *if* one could know everything about the universe at any given moment, one would know everything about any previous state of the universe, and be able to predict everything about any future state (Laplace, 1814/2007). It is important to note that determinism connotes two related, but not identical or mutually dependent, concepts — causality and prediction.

In 1927 Heisenberg showed that it is in principle impossible to know everything about any given moment of the universe because it is in principle impossible to measure the simultaneous position and momentum (and other conjugate variables) of a particle. Some physicists and philosophers thereafter made the mistake of concluding that this limitation somehow exempts the particle from being governed by causality, and renders its behavior *uncertain.* However, not knowing the simultaneous position and momentum of a particle forms no basis for logically concluding that its behavior is either caused or uncaused, or uncertain, and one's ignorance or uncertainty about the behavior of the particle in no way justifies a claim that the particle is behaving in an ignorant or uncertain manner.

What is known, however, is that the change in the momentum of the measured particle was *caused* by its interaction with the measuring particle. This is known unequivocally because the causal relation is a result of HUP. If the measuring particle did not cause a change in the momentum of the measured particle, as stipulated by HUP, one could, in fact, simultaneously measure the position and momentum of a particle. While it describes the prohibition of simultaneous position/momentum measurement of an individual particle mathematically by invoking Planck's constant, HUP depends on causality in order to physically prohibit such measurement. One can understand the causal behavior of individual particles by examining why HUP prohibits the precise simultaneous measurement of their position and momentum.

When one fires a high-energy, short-wavelength photon at another particle, one can precisely measure the particle's position, but knowledge of its momentum becomes imprecise because the collision changes the particle's momentum. When one fires a low-energy, long-wavelength photon at the particle, one can precisely measure its momentum, but knowledge of its position is imprecise due to the photon's longer wavelength. There is nothing about these interactions, nor about HUP's prohibitions, that suggest they occur in an uncaused manner. In fact, a necessary result of HUP is that the change in the measured particle's momentum is *caused* by the interaction. Both macro and quantum events are governed by the law of cause and effect.

One can understand the ubiquitous nature of the causality inherent in determinism through its most general application, "We ought then to regard the present state of the universe as the effect of its anterior state and the cause of the one which is to follow." (Laplace, 1814/2007, p. 4). Knowledge of the universe begins with the Big Bang, and its second moment was caused by that initial event. Its state during the third moment was caused most proximately by its second state, and most fundamentally by the Big Bang. Moving forward, its third state caused its fourth, its fourth, its fifth, and through this chain of cause and effect, the universe arrived at its present state.

This state-by-state evolution of the universe *completely* describes the causal mechanism involved, and also governs all events occurring within. For example, any specific event *within* the second moment of the universe was caused by the Big Bang event. Thus every human decision is caused by antecedent states of the universe that originated with, and were determined by, that event. A freely willed decision must be free from the determination of any entity, event, or process over which the human has no control. Because humans controlled neither the Big Bang nor the causality by which the universe evolved, one cannot fundamentally attribute human actions to a human will, let alone a free will.

Causality is, in fact, so fundamental a universal process that it is a priori. This understanding is made clear by the following argument. The first priori fact is that the universe exists, and the second is that it changes. Change is *the* fundamental universal process, without which all would remain eternally still. There would have been no Big Bang, and no formation of galaxies, stars and planets. Without change, absolutely nothing would happen.

What is change? The universe is comprised of mass-energy, and the forces that act upon it, and can be described as particles moving through space. At one moment, each particle occupies a specific point within the universe. The first known instance of change occurred as the potential energy of the Big Bang became the kinetic energy that, as momentum, propelled each particle to a different position during the universe's second moment. As the universe changed from its initial state to its state at the next moment, each particle also manifested this change. Change is therefore expressed by the universe manifesting a certain state at one moment, and a different state at the next, and each particle within manifesting a certain position at one moment, and a different position at the next.

Understanding that momentum *causes* the universe's expansion and mass-energy's motion reveals that causality is the process by which change occurs. Change requires causality, and because it occurs in both macro and quantum phenomena, nature is a priori causal.

A priori causality is not just fundamental to nature; it is also fundamental to science. Scientific method requires causality to undergird the "same cause, same effect" principle indispensable to ascertaining scientific knowledge through experimental replication. Without causality, there would be no science. *Therefore, categorically and in principle, an a priori universal causality founded on the a priori process of change cannot be successfully challenged through any manner of empirical evidence considered within a scientific method that requires causality in order to arrive at a hypothesis.* Universal causality is also evidenced by the law of conservation of momentum that governs both macro and quantum levels of nature. Because canonical momentum is never created or lost in particle collisions, the gain or loss in the canonical momentum of one particle is *caused* by its interaction with the other.

Some free will defenses describe decisions as numinous, spiritual, or non-physical, suggesting that they are thereby exempt from physical law. The problem for these arguments is that there is a precise moment within the 13.7 billion-year universal timeline wherein a decision occurs. Because time is not independent of, (cannot exist without) motion, and motion is not independent of space, "numinous" human decisions *are*, in fact, subject to physical law, and are therefore prohibited by causality from being freely willed.

Suggestions that quantum events occur in an indeterministic, or uncaused, manner are based on ignorance of their causes. One cannot precisely predict the rate of decay of a single radioactive isotope, and this has led some to wrongly conclude that radioactive decay is therefore random in the strong sense of having no cause. Similarly flawed conclusions include the assertion that the inability to simultaneously measure the position and momentum of a particle as prohibited by HUP means that such particle behavior is uncaused, and that ignorance of aspects of particle behavior in the double-slit experiment and in entanglement means that the behavior is uncaused. While the causal mechanisms of the above phenomena are, and may forever remain, unknown, this ignorance does not justify a conclusion that they are uncaused.

By the early twentieth century, it was clear that Newton's classical mechanics could not provide a complete methodology for precisely measuring and predicting the behavior of individual particles. Classical measurement and prediction of macro objects requires the precise and simultaneous measurement of their position and momentum, and this can be done without probability equations because at the macro level the uncertainties imposed by HUP are so small as to be insignificant. These uncertainties, however, become much larger and prohibitive in the quantum world. Because one cannot simultaneously measure the position and momentum of a single particle precisely enough to render accurate predictions solely through classical mechanics, one must rely on both classical and quantum mechanics to predict individual particle behavior.

Quantum mechanics relies on probabilities to predict the behavior of individual particles, leading some to speculate that free will might somehow arise probabilistically. However, the probability equations used in quantum prediction are derived from the prior deterministic, non-stochastic, measurement of groups of particles that behave causally. Initially, through deterministic, classical mechanics, one repeatedly measures the simultaneous position and momentum of *groups* of particles. These classical measurements form the dataset for, and are indispensable to, deriving the probability equations used in quantum prediction. The probabilities could not be derived were the groups of particles forming the dataset behaving acausally.

3. Refutation of Published Free Will Defenses

Having described why causality prohibits free will, I now apply this refutation to arguments put forth in recent articles defending free will.

Baumeister (2008) frames the question as:

> [I]s the person an autonomous entity who genuinely chooses how to act from among multiple options? Or, is the person essentially just one link in a causal chain, so that the person's actions are merely the inevitable product of lawful causes stemming from prior events, and no one could ever have acted differently than how he or she actually did? (p. 14).

For his first defense, Baumeister appeals to the *Principle of Alternate Possibilities*, (PAP) (Frankfurt 2003) and argues that "life is a series of choice points, and at each choice point, you could have chosen differently than you did." (p. 14). This defense invites two interpretations, however neither allows for a free will.

One could answer "No, you could not have chosen differently than you did." This is a *real world* refutation of the PAP challenge. Because there is one known universe, there is one universal chain of causality that, as explained, governs the universe and every event within. To posit otherwise is to suggest that natural events like human decisions can occur outside of the universe, or circumvent its state-by-state evolution. One could alternately answer his question in the affirmative: "Yes, you could have chosen differently than you did," but only hypothetically. One could have chosen differently *if* the universe and one's life had evolved differently, or *if* one lived in a different universe. They did not, and one does not.

He next appeals to Kant's (1797/1967) version of free will that is limited to instances where humans are, in Baumeister's words, "acting in a morally virtuous manner based on enlightened reasoning." (p. 14). However, because they have causal antecedents that regress to the Big Bang, such decisions are not freely willed.

Baumeister (2008) asserts "Free will should be understood not as the starter or motor of action but rather as a passenger who occasionally grabs the steering wheel or even as just the navigator who says to turn left up ahead." (p. 14). However, the causal principle permits no such interference. To illustrate, causality uncompromisingly stipulates that the first in a series of even a quadrillion dominoes determines and explains the toppling of the quadrillionth. It neither allows nor requires the break or interference with a causal chain that is postulated by Baumeister. He next references Gollwitzer, (1999) and suggests that "free will would have more to do with deciding (now) to walk to the store when the rain stops (later) than with directing each footstep during the actual trip." (Baumeister, 2008, p. 15). He argues that if a decision is about a future action, it escapes causality, however, causal law makes no such allowance.

Proposing that the waning of self-control subsequent to its exercise during a previous task is due to the waning of free will, he cites an experiment by Gailliot, Baumeister, DeWall, Ma-ner, Plant, et al. (2007) suggesting that through raising blood glucose levels by drinking lemonade, one can regain a measure of the depleted free will. However, because the drinking of lemonade is entirely deterministic, the action can in no way be described as having been freely willed.

Fingarette (2008) claims that determinism is irrelevant to whether humans choose freely, and deems the matter moot, asserting "I cannot live my life on a deterministic basis. Nor can you. If you are alive, you are conscious of making choices." (p. 3). According to Breer (1989), Pereboom (2001), Blackmore (2005) and this author, however, it is possible to integrate the understanding that one's choices are deterministic. Integrating the perspective is as straightforward as actively reminding oneself of the causal nature of one's choices, and shifting one's cognitive and emotional responses to reflect the corollary that, in their conventional application, personal blame, guilt, arrogance and envy do not any longer make sense. One's personal morality is thus guided not by fundamental attribution, but by an ever-present awareness that actions have helpful and harmful consequences.

His more direct challenge to determinism questions the "I" that chooses, however, because the causal antecedents to a choice span back to before the chooser's birth, no conceptualization of a personal "I" can justify fundamentally attributing choices to humans. Nor does his distinction between a "passive" and an "active" aspect of consciousness rescue free will, as choices by either aspect would be causal. His last challenge to determinism suggests that causality does not prevent humans from doing what they want: "The determinist emphasizes that our wants have causes. This is an important issue. But it is a different issue from whether we are able to do what we want." (Fingarette, 2008, p. 5). This claim fails to recognize that because the causal antecedents to every human want span back to the Big Bang, humans actually do what *it* wanted.

Relying on Cartesian dualism, Meyer (2011) writes: "Indeed, material determinism fails to acknowledge the numinous qualities of the mind and thus threatens to change what it means to be human." (p. 85). However, as explained, ascribing non-physicality to the human mind and choices does not help because choices necessarily occupy specific moments in time, and are therefore woven into the state-by-state causal evolution of the physical universe.

Referencing Ellis, he next suggests that quantum mechanics can rescue free will, and contends that "the constituent particles at the micro-level, albeit devoid of individual properties as such, are influenced by extrinsic factors that modify their native indeterminacy and give rise to 'entangled states' that would allow for the emergence of free will." (Meyer, 2011, p. 90). This does not, however, solve his problem because the extrinsic factors are causal. Nor does his appeal to entangled states help. Entanglement is a mystery, revealing that particles at a distance instantaneously exchange information, however, such behavior would in no way thereby allow for a free will.

Challenging Wegner's (2002) assertion that conscious will is an illusion, Meyer cites learning to control some unconscious actions like heart rate and blood pressure, and learning to direct thoughts away from obsessive patterns of cognition, panic attacks, and bouts of depression as voluntary mechanisms. However, unconscious actions, obsessive patterns, panic attacks and depression all have causal antecedents, as would any efforts to control and direct them, and are thus not freely willed.

Mele (2012) claims that "scientists – neuro-scientists and others – have not proved that free will is an illusion and have not provided powerful evidence for that claim." (p. 422). In truth, because science shows that causality is a priori, not only does science provide devastating evidence against free will, it does so through unimpeachable means.

He asks which conception of free will empirical evidence refutes. Noting that a priori knowledge supersedes empirical evidence, causality refutes any and all conceptions that attribute it to humans. His voicing the Compatibilist contention that "as long as the causal chain goes through the agent in an appropriate way, the agent can exercise free will," (Mele, 2012, p. 434) suggests an inaccurate understanding of causality. If one lined up one hundred dominoes, for example, and tilted the first so that it caused the second to tumble, and this second domino caused the third to tumble, and so on, causality does not allow for an "appropriate way" by which the ninety-ninth domino could, free from the effect of the ninety-eight antecedent dominoes, tumble the one hundredth. An agent can neither circumvent nor assume authorship of an action compelled upon it by antecedent causes.

Seeking free will within tie-breaking mech-anisms, Mele (2012) asserts: "Even if some action-ties are broken for us unconsciously well before we are aware of what we 'intend' to do, it certainly does not follow from this that we never make effective conscious decisions." (p. 435). Intentions, however, do not possess a unique characteristic that exempts them from causality. He next contends: "Whereas the laws of nature that apply to deterministic causation are exceptionless, those that apply most directly to indeterministic causation are instead probabilistic," (p. 435) suggesting that perhaps probabilities rescue free will. His mistake here is in confusing the mechanics used to predict quantum behavior with the governance of particles by the principle of causality. He posits that "Moe's decision to help a stranded motorist is indeterministically caused by, among other things, his thinking that he should help," (p. 435) however, while one might, (if it could ever be done) use quantum probabilities to predict that decision, it would not be the probabilistic mechanics of the prediction, but rather the decision's causal nature, that would prohibit the decision from being freely willed.

He next suggests: "In agent causation, an agent is connected by the relation causation to an action (or intention) and that connection is not reducible to a connection between states or events and the action (or intention)." (Mele, 2012, p. 436). He is claiming that while a person may cause an action, causality does not explain the action the person caused. There are two ways to refute this claim. The first is to categorically reject the idea that a person can cause an action or event in a way that is unexplained by prior states of the universe. The second is to note that the idea of a person causing an action acausally is incoherent. His claim that intentional actions can arise without their having been caused combines the notion that intentions are exempt from causality with the idea that an uncaused intention can be attributed to a human, and also lacks coherence.

4. Implications of Free Will Belief and Disbelief

Libet, Gleason, Wright and Pearl (1983) published findings suggesting that the unconscious has already initiated motor activity several hundred ms before subjects reported a conscious awareness of their decision to move their finger and/or wrist. A recent replication by Fried, Mukamel and Kreiman (2011) validated the results while another suggests that unconscious activity can precede conscious awareness of decisions by as much as ten s (Soon, Brass, Heinze, Haynes, et al., 2008). Bargh, Chen and Burrows (1996) and subsequent replications strengthened the empirical challenge to free will through priming experiments where subjects were unconsciously induced toward various behaviors without their awareness of the manipulation.

Vohs and Schooler (2008) became concerned that as people abandon the belief in free will, their moral behavior may be compromised. Utilizing the priming protocol, the researchers conducted experiments that induced disbelief in free will in subjects to see how this might influence cheating behavior. In one experiment, half of the subjects read a passage from Crick's *The Astonishing Hypothesis* (1994) that included such phrases as; "'You,' your joys and your sorrows, your memories and your ambitions, your sense of personal identity and free will, are in fact no more than the behavior of a vast assembly of nerve cells and their associated molecules," and "You're nothing but a pack of neurons." (p. 3) The other half read a passage not related to human will. After twenty trials the researchers found that subjects in the unfree will belief group cheated an average of twelve times while subjects in the control group cheated an average of nine times.

However, while they tested to ensure the passages did not alter affect, the researchers neglected to test how they might alter self-identity and world-view. I contend that phrases like, "You're nothing but a pack of neurons" could induce not negative affect, but rather indifference. The priming likely divested the unfree will belief group of a measure of their humanity. My stronger criticism is that while they primed subjects to disbelieve in free will, the researchers did not concurrently prime the essential caveat that this understanding does not thereby grant one license to do as one pleases. Omitting this precept, I contend, is like teaching drivers to push a gas pedal and turn a steering wheel, but neglecting to teach them to apply the brakes. Also, in their second experiment, the researchers used language that primed moral behavior in the free will belief group, but not in the unfree will belief group. The free will belief group was instructed to read Velton-type (1968) statements that included, "Avoiding temptation requires that I exert my free will." (Vohs and Schooler, 2008, p. 51). The unfree will belief group, however, read statements like, "A belief in free will contradicts the known facts that the universe is governed by lawful principles of science." (p. 51). The subjects were not concurrently primed that, for example, humans are conditioned by parents and society toward moral behavior. I contend that equivalent, or no, morality-relevant statements in the text the two groups read would have minimized or eliminated the found disparity.

More important than these methodological flaws, the researchers focused on the relatively innocuous and victimless crime of cheating in an experiment. Because free will belief encourages a rational attribution of immoral behavior to humans (i.e., blaming), unyielding, aggressive, and criminal responses to such behavior would be more prevalent with free will believers than with those who hold free will to be an illusion. Research suggests attributive blaming correlates with

   a. more aggressive and violent seeking of revenge and retribution (Folger and Baron, 1996; Wickens, Wiesenthal, Flora and Flett, 2011);

b. less forgiveness (Bradfield and Aquino, 1999; Meneses and Greenberg, 2011);

c. more interpersonal conflict (Cashmore, and Parkinson, 2011; DeBoard-Lucas, Fosco, Raynor, and Grych, 2010; Meneses and Greenberg);

d. less compassion (Decety, Echols and Correll, 2010; Zucker and Weiner, 1993);

e. less charity (Campbell, Carr and MacLachlan, 2001; Carr and MacLachlan, 1998; Cheung and Chan, 2000);

f. more anger toward others (Csibi and Csibi, 2011; Decety, Echols and Correll; Martinko and Zellars, 1998; Meneses and Greenberg);

g. more anxiety and depression (Csibi and Csibi; DeBoard-Lucas, Fosco, Raynor, and Grych; Fourie, Rauch, Morgan, Ellis, Jordaan and Thomas, 2011; O'Connor, Kotze and Wright, 2011; Raskauskas, 2010);

h. more arrogance and belittling of others (Decety, Echols and Correll; Miceli and Castelfranchi, 2011; O'Connor, Kotze and Wright);

and

i. more self-blame and guilt (Csibi and Csibi; Fourie, Rauch, Morgan, Ellis, Jordaan and Thomas; de Guzman, et.al., 2010; Ni-colle, Bach, Frith and Dolan, 2011; O'Connor, Kotze and Wright).

Interviewing persons convicted of crimes against persons known to them would likely reveal that stronger belief in free will correlates highly with each of these responses.

5. Free Will Belief and Climate Change Denial

Free will belief also contributes to climate change denial. A correlate to free will belief is that humans are fundamentally, as distinct from pragmatically, responsible for their actions. Pew Research Center (2014) reported that Americans ranked global warming near the bottom of Presidential and Congressional priorities for the years 2009 through 2014, and that only 44 percent of Americans currently believe there is solid evidence the phenomenon exists and is anthropomorphic. Seeking a partial explanation for this indifference and denial, Crompton and Kasser (2010) cited evidence that individuals overcome guilt about global warming by denying their actions, refusing to care, and shifting the blame to others. In her study of Norwegian villagers relatively well informed about climate change, Norgaard (2009) found that individuals reported feeling guilty about over-consuming resources and "being a bad person." (p. 32).

Guilt is a self-attribution that requires a belief in free will. Because it is more difficult to rationally feel guilty about behavior over which one believes one has no control, guilt-induced climate change denial is fueled by free will belief.

Individuals whose self-identity is threatened by climate change information reduce the threat by redefining or dismissing the information. Gecas and Burke (1995) suggested that the need to preserve a positive self-concept leads individuals to avoid or selectively accept threatening information, and to work hard to not change their identity. Norgaard (2009) found that individuals re-define situations that threaten self-identity, and Baumeister (1998) reported that individuals dismiss such information. Because positive self-identity is largely predicated on a favorable evaluation of one's personal morality, and the personal morality construct is dependent on the idea of free will, identity-based redefinition and dismissal of climate change information is also attributable to free will belief.

Crompton and Kasser (2010) recommended the practice of mindfulness, described as "a non-judgmental awareness of one's experiences," (p. 26) for one to manage environmental threats to identity, and referenced Brown and Kasser (2005), who found that the practice is empirically associated with positive environmental behavior. Mindfulness practice cultivates through meditation and intent the same attitude of non-judgment that disbelief in free will cultivates through rational assessment. As one deepens one's understanding of the implications of free will being an illusion, it becomes increasingly difficult to rationally blame others and oneself for held attitudes and expressed behaviors. Freeing oneself of assumed fundamental moral responsibility with its often paralyzing sense of accountability may make it easier to more positively respond to climate change through an empowering attitude of genuine concern.

Kellstedt, Zahran, and Vedlitz (2008) found that helplessness also induced climate change denial. This mechanism is insidious in that the better informed individuals are about climate change, the more helpless they tend to feel, and the greater their need to deny the threat. Individuals value the feeling of efficacy free will belief can foster. Free will belief likely conditions individuals to maintain a sense of fundamental efficacy and, notwithstanding its illusory nature, avoid or deny circumstances that threaten the attitude. Overcoming free will belief may allow individuals to better accept their fundamental, as distinct from pragmatic, helplessness, and thereby reduce their need to deny climate change. While overcoming free will belief would not be easy, humanity may find this fundamental restructuring of human psychology useful. As the world experiences increased climate change impacts, guilt, blame and helplessness may increase, and induce greater denial in a downward spiral. While there are other causes of climate change denial, free will belief-based denial may render humanity psychologically less capable of confronting them.

6. Conclusion

Understanding the causal nature of human will opens up expansive new areas of research. Foremost, what benefits might accrue from humanity overcoming free will belief? Which attitudes and behaviors would then change within personal, interpersonal, societal, and international domains, and in what ways would they change under this new paradigm? The universe has condemned over one billion humans to extreme poverty, and has compelled humans to inflict extreme and unnatural pain on tens of billions of food and laboratory animals each year. To what extent does belief in fundamental personal responsibility, and the denial it encourages, substantially explain this cruelty? How do researchers test the effects of individuals and societies as they move away from free will belief?

Other questions are less pragmatic, however profoundly relate to our shared human experience.

What evolutionary purpose might the belief in free will have served, and what was the origin of our desire and need to consider ourselves autonomous agents? How does the world acknowledging free will as an illusion constitute a bigger revolution in human thought than was brought about by Einstein and other top scientists? What effect would the understanding that we humans manifest the universe's *will*, rather than an autonomous will, have on our human identity?

Some contend that the question of whether humans have a free will has not yet been settled. However, as with evolution, notwithstanding the widespread public denial and dismissal of preponderant scientific evidence supporting the theory, the causal nature of human will was understood long ago. As noted by the distinguished British physicist, astronomer and mathematician, Sir James Jeans (1943/1981):

> Practically all modern philosophers of the first rank — Descartes, Spinoza, Leibniz, Locke, Hume, Kant, Hegel, Mill, Alexander, as well as many others — have been determinists in the sense of admitting the cogency of the arguments for determinism, but many have at the same time been indeterminists in the sense of hoping to find a loophole of escape from these arguments. Often they conceded that our apparent freedom is an illusion, so that the only loophole they could hope to find would be an

explanation as to how the illusion could originate.

An understanding of the a priori nature of causality may finally establish a firm consensus within the sciences that free will is an illusion. More important than understanding why the universe for millennia compelled upon humanity this illusion, future research might aim to better understand the incorrect and motivated reasoning behind the belief, and how it might be overcome. The question of the nature of human will is no small matter. It is one of appearance vs. reality, of effects and their causes, and of how humanity's compelled actions in the present will likely shape the fate of life on the planet for the next century and beyond.

References

Bargh, J. A., Chen, M., & Burrows, L. (1996). Automaticity of social behavior: direct effects of trait construct and stereotype activation on action. *Journal of Personality and Social Psychology*, Vol. 71, No. 2. 230-244.

Baumeister, R. F., Dale, K., & Sommer, K. L. (1998). Freudian defense mechanisms and empirical findings in modern social psychology: Reaction formation, projection, displacement, undoing, isolation, sublimation, and denial. *Journal of Personality*, *66*(6), 1081-1124.

Baumeister, R. F. (2008). Free will in scientific psychology. *Perspectives on   Psychological Science*, 3:14·9.

Blackmore, S. (2005). *Conversations on consciousness.* Oxford University Press.

Bradfield, M., & Aquino, K. (1999). The effects of blame attributions and offender likableness on forgiveness and revenge in the workplace. *Journal of Management*, 25(5), 607-631.

Breer, P. (1989). *The spontaneous self: viable alternatives to free will*. Institute for Naturalistic Philosophy.

Brown, K. W., & Kasser, T. (2005). Are psychological and ecological well-being compatible? The role of values, mindfulness, and lifestyle. *Social Indicators Research*, 74(2), 349-368.

Campbell, D., Carr, S. C., & MacLachlan, M. (2001). Attributing "Third World Poverty" in Australia and Malawi: A Case of Donor Bias? 1. *Journal of Applied Social Psychology*, 31(2), 409-430.

Carr, S. C., & MacLachlan, M. (1998). Actors, observers, and attributions for Third World poverty: Contrasting perspectives from Malawi and Australia. *The Journal of social psychology*, 138(2), 189-202.

Cashmore, J. A., & Parkinson, P. N. (2011). Reasons for disputes in high conflict families. *Journal of Family Studies*, 17(3), 186-203.

Cheung, C. K., & Chan, C. M. (2000). Social-cognitive factors of donating money to charity, with special attention to an international relief organization. *Evaluation and Program Planning*, 23(2), 241-253.

Crick, F. (1994). *The astonishing hypothesis*. Scribners.

Crompton, T., & Kasser, T. (2010). Human identity: a missing link in environmental campaigning. *Environment, 52*(4), 23-33.

Csibi, S., & Csibi, M. (2011). Study of aggression related to coping, self-appreciation and social support among adolescents. *Nordic Psychology, 63*(4), 35.

DeBoard-Lucas, R. L., Fosco, G. M., Raynor, S. R., & Grych, J. H. (2010). Interparental conflict in context: Exploring relations between parenting processes and children's conflict appraisals. *Journal of Clinical Child & Adolescent Psychology, 39*(2), 163-175.

Decety, J., Echols, S., & Correll, J. (2010). The blame game: the effect of responsibility and social stigma on empathy for pain. *Journal of Cognitive Neuroscience, 22*(5), 985-997.

Ellis, G. F. (2001). Quantum theory and the macroscopic world. *Quantum mechanics. Scientific perspectives on divine action, 5*, 259-291.

Fingarette, H. (2008). Free choice. *Current Psychology, 27*(1), 1-5.

Folger, R., & Baron, R. A. (1996). Violence and hostility at work: A model of reactions to perceived injustice.

Fourie, M. M., Rauch, H. G., Morgan, B. E., Ellis, G. F., Jordaan, E. R., & Thomas, K. G. (2011). Guilt and pride are heartfelt, but not equally so. *Psychophysiology, 48*(7), 888-899.

Frankfurt, H. (2003). Alternate possibilities and moral responsibility. In Gary Watson, ed. 2nd ed., *Free will*, Oxford University Press 169.

Fried, I., Mukamel, R., & Kreiman, G. (2011). Internally generated preactivation of single neurons in human medial frontal cortex predicts volition. *Neuron, 69*(3), 548-562.

Gailliot, M.T., Baumeister, R.F., DeWall, C.N., Maner, J.K., Plant, E.A., Tice, D.M., et al. (2007). Self-control relies on glucose as a limited energy source: Willpower is more than a metaphor. *Journal of Personality and Social Psychology*, 92, 325-336.

Gecas, V., & Burke, P. J. (1995). Self and identity. *Sociological perspectives on social psychology*, 41-67.

Gollwitzer, P.M. (1999). Implementation intentions: Strong effects of simple plans. *American Psychologist*, 54, 493–503.

de Guzman, A. B., Sindac, L. A. G., Sioson, J. J. T., Sison, K. J. B., Socia, J. K. M., Solidum, R. F., ... & Suaberon, L. C. D. (2010). Looking Through a Window: The Guilt and Remorse Space of a Lung Cancer Patient. *Journal of Cancer Education, 25*(4), 663-665.

Heisenberg, W. (1927). On the physical content of the quantum theoretical kinematics and mechanics. (Über den anschaulichen Inhalt der quantentheoretischen Kinematik und

Mechanik). *Zeitschrift fur Physik* 43 (3-4): 172-198.

Jeans, J. H. (1943/1981). *Physics and philosophy.* Dover Publications. 205.

Kant, I. (1797/1967). *Critique of practical reason* (Kritik der praktischen Vernunft). Felix Meiner Verlag.

Kellstedt, P. M., Zahran, S., & Vedlitz, A. (2008). Personal efficacy, the information environment, and attitudes toward global warming and climate change in the United States. *Risk Analysis, 28*(1), 113-126.

Laplace, P. S. (1814/2007). *Pierre-Simon Laplace Philosophical Essay on Probabilities.* Cosimo, Inc.

Libet, B., Gleason, C. A., Wright, E. W., & Pearl, D. K. (1983). Time of conscious intention to act in relation to onset of cerebral activity (readiness-potential) The unconscious initiation of a freely voluntary act. *Brain, 106*(3), 623-642.

Martinko, M. J., & Zellars, K. L. (1998). Toward a theory of workplace violence and aggression: A cognitive appraisal perspective.

Mele, A. (2012). Another scientific threat to free will? *Monist* 95, 422-440.

Meneses, C. W., & Greenberg, L. S. (2011). The Construction of a Model of the Process of Couples' Forgiveness in Emotion-Focused Therapy for Couples. *Journal of marital and family therapy, 37*(4), 491-502.

Meyer, J. R. (2011). Is free will an illusion? *Ethics & Medicine*, Vol. 27, No. 2

Miceli, M., & Castelfranchi, C. (2011). Forgiveness: A Cognitive-Motivational Anatomy. *Journal for the Theory of Social Behaviour*, 41(3), 260-290.

Newton, I. (1687/2010) *The principia: mathematical principles of natural philosophy* (Philosophiae naturalis principia mathematica). Snowball Publishing.

Nicolle, A., Bach, D. R., Frith, C., & Dolan, R. J. (2011). Amygdala involvement in self-blame regret. *Social neuroscience*, 6(2), 178-189.

Norgaard, K. M. (2009). Cognitive and Behavioral Challenges in Responding to Climate Change.

O'Connor, N., Kotze, B., & Wright, M. (2011). Blame and accountability 1: understanding blame and blame pathologies. *Australian Psychiatry*, 19(2), 113-118.

Pereboom, D. (2001). *Living without free will.* Cambridge University Press.

Pew Research Center (2014). Climate Change: Key Data Points from Pew Research: The American public routinely ranks dealing with global warming low on its list of priorities for the president and Congress. This year, it ranked second to last among 20 issues tested. http://www.pewresearch.org/key-data-points/climate-change-key-data-points-from-pew-research/. Retrieved April 15, 2014.

Raskauskas, J. (2010). Multiple peer victimization among elementary school students: relations with social-emotional problems. *Social Psychology of Education*, 13(4), 523-539.

Soon, C., Brass, M., Heinze, H., Haynes, J. (2008). Unconscious determinants of free decisions in the human brain, *Nature Neuroscience* 11 (5): 543-545.

Strawson, G. (1994). The impossibility of ultimate responsibility, *Philosophical Studies*, 75:5-24.

Velten, E. (1968). A laboratory task for the induction of mood states. *Behavioral Research and Therapy*, 6, 607-617.

Vohs, K., Schooler, J. (2008). The value of believing in free will: encouraging a belief in determinism increases cheating, *Psychological Science*, 19: 49-54.

Wegner, D. (2002). *The illusion of conscious will*, MIT Press.

Wickens, C. M., Wiesenthal, D. L., Flora, D. B., & Flett, G. L. (2011). Understanding driver anger and aggression: attributional theory in the driving environment. *Journal of experimental psychology: applied*, 17(4), 354.

Zucker, G. S., & Weiner, B. (1993). Conservatism and Perceptions of Poverty: An Attributional Analysis1. *Journal of Applied Social Psychology*, 23(12), 925-943.

Made in the USA
Charleston, SC
07 May 2014